QUICKBOOKS

The Beginners Ultimate Guide to Learning QuickBooks in Best Optimal Way

LUCAS
CALDERON

Copyright © 2019 Lucas Calderon

All rights reserved.

It is not legal to reproduce, duplicate, or transmit any part of this document by either electronic means or in printed format. Recording of this publication is strictly prohibited

Disclaimer

The information in this book is based on personal experience and anecdotal evidence. Although the author has made every attempt to achieve an accuracy of the information gathered in this book, they make no representation or warranties concerning the accuracy or completeness of the contents of this book. Your circumstances may not be suited to some illustrations in this book.

The author disclaims any liability arising directly or indirectly from the use of this book. Readers are encouraged to seek accounting, legal, or professional help when required.

This guide is for informational purposes only, and the author does not accept any responsibilities for any liabilities resulting from the use of this information. While every attempt has been made to verify the information provided here, the author cannot assume any responsibility for errors, inaccuracies or omission.

Printed in the United States of America

TABLE OF CONTENTS

INTRODUCTION i

CHAPTER ONE - How To Set-up QuickBooks 1

- Set-up Company File: 2
  - If you Select Express Start, then: 4
- Customize QuickBooks For Your Business: 14
  - Charts of Accounts: 15
  . Customize the Icon Bar: 17
  - Download Transaction Online Into QuickBooks: 17
  - Link Your Email To QuickBooks: 19
  - Edit Your QuickBooks Preferences: 20
  - Use QuickBooks Memorized Transactions and Reports: 21
- Learn About The QuickBooks Homepage. 21
- Set-up Your Customers, Vendors, and Jobs: 23
  - Create "Customers" in QuickBooks: 23
  - Create "Jobs" in QuickBooks: 29
  - Create a "Vendor" in QuickBooks: 31

CHAPTER TWO - Manage Your Banking Transactions... 36
- Link Your Bank Accounts:.......................... 36
- Import, Match and Add Transactions 37
- Record All Your Bank Transfer and Deposits:.. 42

CHAPTER THREE - Manage Your Business Credit Card Transactions 44
- Create a Reconciliation of Business Credit Card... 44

CHAPTER FOUR-Manage Your Sales and Income With QuickBooks.. 47
- How To Create and Send Invoices?.......... 47
- Receive Payments..................................... 49
- How To Create and Send Sales Receipts?51
- How To Customize Your Sales Forms 53

CHAPTER FIVE- Manage Your Bills and Other Expenses 54
- Set-up Vendor Center............................... 54
  - How To Create a Bill? 54
  - Enter Expense Type as per the Transaction 56
  - How To Pay Multiple Bills? 58
  - How to Create a Check to Pay the Bill?. 59
  - How To Print Check Bills in Batch? 62

CHAPTER SIX - Financial Reporting 64

- Profit and Loss Statement 64
- Balance Sheet 69
- Manage Accounts Receivable 70
  - Summary of Sales by Customers 70
  - Details of Sales by Customers 72
  - Details on Unbilled Charges: 73
- Manage Accounts Payables 74
  - Summary of Accounts Payables: 74
  - Review Purchases and Other Expenses: 75
  - Transaction List by Vendor: 76
- Manage Payrolls: 77
- Manage Sales tax: 79
- Inventory and Finished Goods Management 79
- Statement of Cash Flows: 80
  - ❏ Cash Flow Forcast Report: 80
  - ❏ Cash Flow Statement For Current Period: 81
  - Aging Analysis of Accounts Receivables and Payables 81

CHAPTER SEVEN - Different Versions of QuickBooks 86
- QuickBooks Self-employed 86
- QuickBooks Online: 88

- Features Of QuickBooks Online: 88
- QuickBooks for Desktop/Mac: 104
  - QuickBooks Pro: 105
  - QuickBooks Premier: 105
  - QuickBooks Enterprise: 106
- QuickBooks Accountant: 107

CHAPTER EIGHT - Key Shortcuts For Using QuickBooks 109

- QuickBooks Desktop (Pro, Premier, Enterprise) 109
  - Open, set up, and close QuickBooks ... 109
  - Navigate around QuickBooks 111
  - Start a new task anywhere in QuickBooks 112
  - Data fields on forms 114
  - Date fields on forms 115
  - Forms and transactions (invoices, expenses, etc) 119
  - Lists (Customer Center, Account Register, Item List, etc) 125
- QuickBooks Desktop for Mac 127
  - Open, set up, and close QuickBooks ... 127
  - Navigate around QuickBooks 128
  - Data fields on forms 130

- 131
  - Date fields on forms 131
  - Forms and transactions (invoices, expenses, etc) 134
  - Lists (Customer Center, Account Register, Item List, etc) 136

CONCLUSION 138
ABOUT THE AUTHOR 140
INDEX 141

INTRODUCTION

Every business irrespective of its size requires maintaining proper accounts on a regular basis. They have to keep track of their bills, expenses, and cash flows. Because the success, as well as the progress of any business, depends more on its financial reporting.

In case you have no idea why am I linking financial reporting or accounts to the success of your business; here is a brief explanation for you. The sole reason for maintaining your proper accounts, keeping track of your inflows and outflows is critical for not only forecasting your future strategies, allocation

Of your resources but it also helps you to make better and wise decisions. With your past financial performance, you can analyze the overall progression or suppression of your business.

I am not going to go into the details of why financial reporting is important as it is not the subject of interest in this book. My discussion is about one of the most amazing and helping accounting software; QuickBooks.

The reason why I am writing a book on this accounting software is that it really helped me keep track of my income and expenses. Whether you are an entrepreneur, company, freelancer or a self-employed person, QuickBooks is a great option for keeping

Track of your money. This software offers brilliant and innovative accounting tools that help you to manage almost all the financial areas of your business/company.

I have tried my best to explain all the features and how to use the accounting tools of QuickBooks in this guide. With the help of this guide, you can explore QuickBooks and its features better and more easily! This guide is quite helpful for all beginners including entrepreneurs, freelancers, single-member companies and even the accounting students.

The secret is to read the chapter and then doing exactly the same practice and trust me by the end of this book you'll learn how to use QuickBooks

CHAPTER ONE - How To Set-up QuickBooks

As you know the features and tools of QuickBooks - the accounting software; it is now time to look at how to use these tools and features for smart accounting. I am going to explain everything step-by-step so that you could easily understand how to use QuickBooks.

But first, let me explain what does setting up QuickBooks means. After you purchase the desired package, the next step is to customize the QuickBooks as per your business/company. You enter the details after which QuickBooks allows you access to other accounting options and tools.

- <u>Set-up Company File:</u>

The first and the most critical step in setting up QuickBooks is the Creation of the Company File. In other words, it is called creating or setting up a new company in QuickBooks. The performance and efficiencies of the whole software depend on how diligently you have created the Company File.

Here are the steps to Create or Set-up the Company File:

1. Open QuickBooks from the QuickBooks desktop.

2. Click on the 'File' option from the QuickBooks menu.
3. Select 'New Company' from the 'File' option.
4. Here you will be provided two options to help you create the Company File:
    a. **Express Start:** Select 'Express Start' in case you want to start right away.
    b. **Detailed Start:** Select 'Detailed Start' in case you want to add all the info in QuickBooks from the beginning.

Express Start is an easy, simple and straight-forward method to create the company file as compared to the 'Detailed Start'. And in my opinion, the 'Express Start' option is more suitable for beginners. Therefore I am going to focus on 'How to create the company file using the Express Start Option' only in this book. Otherwise, the detailed start will only confuse and make it hard for you to understand the basics of QuickBooks.

- If you Select Express Start, then:

    5. You will see a dialog box with three steps, fill the required information in three steps.
    6. **'Tell Us About Your Business'**: Here you are required to enter the relevant information about your company. Once you enter the

name, industry, type, and tax ID of your company then click 'continue'.

7. **'Enter Your Business Contact Info'**: this is the step where you enter the legal name of your business and its general contact information.

    a. Step '7' is the one that leads you to the creation of your company file. But before you click on the 'Create File' button. First, click the 'Preview Your Settings' button.

    b. In the 'Preview Your Setting' menu, click on the 'Charts of Accounts' button.

c. A list of accounts will be opened under the 'Chart of Accounts'. It is a list of all the common accounts as relevant to your industry. Here you will see that some accounts are already 'Checked'. These are the accounts which are proposed by QuickBooks to be included in your Charts. You can uncheck these accounts if you want.

d. Review the list of the accounts and check or uncheck the appropriate account boxes that you want to add or remove. Simply just click on the unchecked or already checked accounts to add or remove.

e. Now click on the other tab that is 'Company File Location' tab. Here you will notice a default location suggested by QuickBooks.

- If you want your files to be saved in a different location, then select 'Change Location', browse/choose the

new location and click 'OK.'
f. Again click 'OK' and you will be redirected to the 'Contact Info' screen.
g. Now click on the 'Create Company File' button.

Congratulations you have created your first 'Company File'. After you have created the company file the next screen will pop up. The following next steps are about adding all the critical information about your business in QuickBooks. Here is how you would do it.

8. A dialogue box 'You've Got a Company File! Now Add Your Info' will pop-up. Here you are

required to enter details of your business at three different levels.

9. Click on the 'Add Info' button in the 'Add the people you do business with' section.

   a. **Choose How to Add**: You will see four different options on how to add information. Select the fourth option 'Paste from Excel or enter manually' and then click 'continue'.

   b. **Select Who to Add**: A dialogue box with a 'Data Entry Table' will be opened. Now choose the contact type such as customer, employee or vendor. Fill in the contact information under the 'Name' field.

c. Add as many contacts as you want to add in the table using the same step 'b'.

d. If you want to enter the opening balances of your contacts (vendors/customers), then click the 'Enter Opening Balances' button. Enter the figures.

e. Once you are finished, click the 'Continue' button to proceed further.

f. **Review and Finish**: Look for any contact that needed to be fixed before you could add it to the table. You can edit the customer/vendor cells easily because they are customizable. Once you have fixed the errors, click 'continue' and proceed. You will be redirected to the same dialogue box as in step 8.
10. Again click 'Add Info' of the 'Add your products and services' section.
    a. Choose a Type: Now select an option either 'service' or 'non-

inventory part'. And click 'continue.'

b. Select What to Add: now add the relevant information in the 'Data Entry Table'. This step is quite similar to step 9b.

c. Click 'Continue'.

d. Review and Finish: Edit or correct any errors before finishing up. Once you are done, click 'continue' again.

11. You will be redirected to the 'You've Got a Company File! Now Add Your Info' again.

12. Now click on 'Add info' of the last section, 'Add bank account information'.
    a. Enter Accounts: Now enter your bank account(s) details in the required field.
    b. Click 'Continue'.
    c. Choose Options: It has some advanced options which are not appropriate at a beginner level. You can explore it anyways.
    d. You can now click 'Start Working' and begin to use QuickBooks. As you have successfully created the Company file.

If you have more than one business or different industries you can create multiple company files using the same steps.

- Customize QuickBooks For Your Business:

Now I am going to explain to you how you can customize this accounting software according to your business type/nature/industry. Here you would need to modify the tools and features as per your needs and how you would want to use them. Basically, QuickBooks customization is for your ease. It includes customizing or modifying various different things such as 'Charts of Accounts', the 'Icon bar' etc.

- **Charts of Accounts:**

You already know how to customize the charts of accounts in the previous chapter. It is the same. To explain to you further, I just want to tell you that there are certain accounts that a business needs to maintain in order to prepare its financial statements. Make sure you select all of the following accounts while creating the company file. These include:

- Business Asset Accounts: This account keeps track of all your intangible, tangible, current and noncurrent assets. This includes cash/bank, fixed assets, and accounts receivable/trade receivables.

- Business Liabilities: here you maintain records of your current and non-current liabilities such as Account payables/trade payables, loans, credit cards, and other liabilities.
- Business Income and Expense Accounts: You need to maintain income, cost of goods sold, expenses, and other income and expense accounts.
- Equity: keeping track of the owner's equity. Recording any addition or withdrawal in equity by the owner or the business.

Customize the Icon Bar:

The main reason for customizing the icon bar is to increase efficiency. It is very simple and easy.

1. Icon bar is right below the menu bar.
2. Right click on the icon bar.
3. Select 'customize icon bar'.
4. Add or remove the icons from the icon bar.

- ## Download Transaction Online Into QuickBooks:

It will reduce the risks of error while inputting transaction data in QuickBooks plus increase efficiency. Usually, most people download banking and credit card transactions. Here is how you do it:

1. Open 'Charts of Accounts'.

2. Right-click on the 'Account' you want to set-up.
3. Click 'edit'.
4. Click 'set up Online Services' on the lower-left corner.
5. Your transactions would be downloaded. After the downloading enter vendor name, expense account, and a memo.

You can download multiple transactions using the same steps. In the beginning, you have to enter details manually but QuickBooks will become smarter progressively and it will memorize the transactions as per the vendor.

- **Link Your Email To QuickBooks:**

Linking your business email to QuickBooks will allow you to send invoices and statements to your customers and key stakeholders. The outcome of this feature is that it will increase your cash inflows and credit your account receivables.

1. From QuickBooks menu tab click 'edit'.
2. Then select 'preferences'. Select the 'My Preferences' tab.
3. Click on 'Send Forms' from the preference tab.
4. Select 'Webmail' under the section 'send e-mail'.
5. Click on 'Add' at the bottom of the screen.

6. Now add the 'Email address' in the address is filed.
7. Select the 'Email Provider' for example G-mail' from the drop-down box.
8. Click 'ok' and you are good to go.

- <u>Edit Your QuickBooks Preferences:</u>
   1. From QuickBooks menu tab click 'edit'.
   2. Then select 'preferences'. A 'my Preferences tab' will open.
   3. A list will open on the left-hand side. Showing a group of preferences. Each preference is editable so customize them as per your needs.

- **Use QuickBooks Memorized Transactions and Reports:**

When you are entering transactions in QuickBooks,

1. From QuickBooks menu tab click 'edit'.
2. Select 'memorize' to save the transaction. Or
3. Press Ctrl+M.

- **Learn About The QuickBooks Homepage**

QuickBooks has a very simple Homepage in which features are shown in the form of charts. You can also customize as per your preferences. It means you can remove all the features that you don't wish to use.

You can customize, Sales Receipts, Statements and Statement Charges, Estimates, Sales Tax, Sales Orders, Inventory, Payroll, and Time Tracking.

1. From QuickBooks menu tab click 'edit'.
2. Then select 'preferences'.
3. Select 'Desktop View' from the list on the left.
4. Select the 'Company Preferences' tab.
5. Select or deselect the features from customer and vendor lists that you want to see on your homepage.
6. Click 'Ok' at the upper right.

Set-up Your Customers, Vendors, and Jobs:

Creating your customers, jobs/projects and vendors list is actually the base for tracking your income and expenses. Plus these are the skeleton of financial statements.

Create "Customers" in QuickBooks:

Create your 'customer' or 'client' list manually using these steps:

1. Select 'customer/client' (customer center) from the Navigation menu on the left.
2. Now choose 'New Customer' or 'Add Client'.
3. Select 'individual' or 'business' from the client/customer type.

- How To Enter/Input Contact Information?

    1. A dialogue box will open now.
    2. Enter the contact details such as name, business type, email-address business name and telephone number in the relevant fields.
    3. In case there is a discount (usually in the case of clients) choose either a direct discount or wholesale discount under QuickBooks Subscription.

- <u>How To Enter/Input Payment Information?</u>

    1. On the 'Customer Info' dialogue box, you will notice 5 tabs on the lower-left corner.
    2. Click on 'Address' and enter the details about the billing address.
    3. Now click on the 'Payment and Billing' tab. Choose the payment method, payment delivery method and enter the term and opening balance.

In Case you have created a client list, then:

4. Under QuickBooks Subscription, click 'Compare' to compare your product prices.
5. Choose your product choice.
6. Select 'Make me the Admin of This client's QuickBooks'.
7. To add a payroll select the '+AddPayroll' option.
8. Click on 'team access' and choose your team members who can access this.

9. Click 'Save' and enter the information in 'Wholesale Billing Information'.

- Specifications About Sale Tax Information Input:

1. Now select the 'Tax' tab on the 'Customer Info' window.

2. Enter the details such as STN number or customer's resale permit information in case your customer is not subjected to Sales tax.

- Additional Customer Contact:

1. Add other additional information about your customers by clicking the 'Additional Info' tab.

2. Add any attachments such as previous invoice etc under 'attachments tab'.

You can review the Customer setup and it will appear as the following in the customer center.

Create your 'customer' via Import from Excel or CSV File:

1. Select 'customer' from the Navigation menu on the left.
2. Click the 'drop-down arrow' on the 'new customer' button.
3. Select 'Import Customers'.
4. Click 'browse' so that you can locate the excel file you want to import.
5. Now select the files of your excel sheet which you want to

correspond with the QuickBooks fields.
6. Review the data and click the 'import' button.

- Create "Jobs" in QuickBooks:

No matter what services or product your business deliver, QuickBooks' Job Tracking feature enables you to analyze your financial performance by job or project. In other words, it is 'Job Costing'.

* How To Create a New Job?
    1. Select 'customer' from the Navigation menu on the left.
    2. From 'Customers and Jobs' list select the 'customer', whom you

desire to create a job from.

3. On the upper left corner of the Customer Center, click the 'new Customer and Job' button.
4. Click on 'Add Job' drop-down arrow.
5. A 'new Job' window is opened now. Enter the job name in the relevant field.
6. Now Click the 'Job Info' tab and enter job description in the relevant field.
7. Now choose the job type either from the drop-down menu or enter

manually from the "Job Type" field.

8. Select 'Job Status' from the drop-down field.
9. Enter the projected 'Start Date' and estimated 'End Date' in relevant fields.
10. Now click 'Ok'
11. Change the project end date on project completion and enter the actual end date.

- Create a "Vendor" in QuickBooks:

Creating a vendor list is the same as creating a customer list. All the steps are similar except in this case you will navigate to the 'Vendor Center.'

1. Navigate to the 'vendor center' from the menu at the left corner.
2. Now choose 'New Vendor'.
3. A dialogue box will open now.
4. Enter the contact details such as name, business type, email-address business name and telephone number in the relevant fields.

- How To Set-up Payments?
    1. On the 'Vendor Info' dialogue box, you will notice 5 tabs on the lower-left corner.
    2. Click on 'Address' and enter the details about the billing address.

3. Now click on the 'Payment and Billing' tab. Choose the payment method, payment delivery method and enter the term and opening balance.

- How To Set-up Sales Tax?
  1. Now select the 'Tax' tab on the 'Vendor Info' window.
  2. Enter the details such as STN number or vendor's resale permit information in case your vendor is not subjected to Sales tax.

- <u>Add Additional Information</u>
    1. Add other additional information about your vendors by clicking the 'Additional Info' tab.
    2. Add any attachments under the 'attachments tab'.

Now review the 'vendor set-up'. It will appear in the vendor as following.

Create your 'Vendor' via Import from Excel or CSV File:

7. Select 'Vendor' from the Navigation menu on the left.
8. Click the 'drop-down arrow' on the 'new vendor' button.
9. Select 'Import Vendors'.

10. Click 'browse' so that you can locate the excel file you want to import.
11. Now select the files of your excel sheet which you want to correspond with the QuickBooks fields.
12. Review the data and click the 'import' button.

CHAPTER TWO - Manage Your Banking Transactions

- ## Link Your Bank Accounts:
    1. From the homepage click on 'Connect Account' under the 'Bank Account' section on the right corner.
    2. This dialogue box will open.
    3. Now enter your username and password.
    4. Click 'Log-in'.
    5. Click the drop-down arrow of 'Account Type' and select all the account types you want to link with QuickBooks.

- Import, Match and Add Transactions

6. QuickBooks will download all transactions from the last 90 days of your accounts. But you have to enter/export the transactions as well.
7. To enter transactions manually
   a. Go to the Accounting center and open 'Charts of Accounts.'
   b. Select the bank or credit account.
   c. Now select 'View register'.
   d. Enter the date of the oldest transaction that is mostly the opening balance.

8. Now sign-in to bank or credit card account and download the transactions.
9. Upload data for Accounts connected to QuickBooks
    a. Navigate to the tab from the menu.
    b. Click on the 'Account' you want to upload transactions.
    c. Click the drop-down arrow on the update button on the right corner and select 'file upload'.
10. Click 'browse' and select the download transactions from your bank.
11. Select the Account type to whom you want to upload

transaction files from QuickBooks Accounts.

12. Click 'Next'.
13. Now follow the instructions on your screen.
14. Back on Bank and Credit Card page, click on the first transaction.it will open the drop-down the details of the transaction.
15. Select the 'find match' option to match the transactions. then click next.
16. Review the transactions and then click 'Let's Go'.

In case you want to change transaction Category or Add a New transaction.

    a. Back on Bank and Credit Card page, click on the

first transaction.it will open the drop-down the details of the transaction.
b. Click on the transaction category drop-down arrow and select the appropriate category.
c. Repeat the same for a new transaction but click the 'Add' button on the right corner of the screen.
d. If the payee of this transaction is also different then click on the 'payee' cell on the left corner of the transaction

e. Click on '+Add New' and enter the new payee and save.

f. In case you have purchased items under different category but in the same single transaction then you can split this transaction as well.

g. Click the 'Split' button on the right of the transaction next to the 'Add' button'.

h. A Split Transaction window will be opened. Now select the select all the categories of the transaction and add the

total spent from each category.
   i. Then click 'Save and Button' on the down-right corner of the window.

- <u>Record All Your Bank Transfer and Deposits:</u>
  1. In case you transfer an amount, paid a bill or lend a loan from your account, then,
     a. Back on Bank and Credit Card page, click on the first transaction.it will open the drop-down the details of the transaction.
     b. Click the drop-down arrow of the deposit button on the left corner.

QuickBooks

    c. Select 'transfer'
2. In the case of Deposits
    a. Repeat the step 1a and 1b.
    b. Select 'Sales receipts'.
    c. Select 'create and then 'bank Deposit.'
    d. Select the 'Account type' from the drop-down menu in which you want to enter the deposit
    e. Select the payments you want to combine.
    f. Then click 'Save and Close' or 'Save and New' in case you want to enter more.

CHAPTER THREE - Manage Your Business Credit Card Transactions

- Create a Reconciliation of Business Credit Card

1. From the Homepage, select 'reconcile' under the banking section.
2. Click on the 'Accounts' drop-down arrow.
3. Select 'Credit Card Account'.
4. Enter the 'credit Card statement date' in the statement date field. And match the opening balance

on credit card statements with QuickBooks.

5. Enter the closing balance of the credit card statement in the Ending Balance field and enter the finance charges if any in the Enter Any Finance Charge section.
6. Now click 'continue'.
7. A Reconcile Window will now open.
8. Check the "Hide Transactions After the Statement's End Date" option.
9. Now click on each transaction that also

appears on your credit card statement.
10. Check for the difference getting to 0.00. It will indicate that your account is successfully reconciled.
11. Click "reconcile now'. A Select Reconciliation Report window will be opened.
12. Now select the type of reconciliation report you want to view and click 'display', 'print' button. Then click the close button.

CHAPTER FOUR-Manage Your Sales and Income With QuickBooks

- How To Create and Send Invoices?

1. Navigate to the customer center (customer) from the QuickBooks homepage.
2. Select 'Invoices' under the 'customers' section.
3. A window 'Invoice' will appear.
4. Enter the customer name, email, billing address, receipt date, reference, and deposit

number and select payment type.

5. Enter other details including product/service name, description, quantity, rate and amount.
6. After entering all the invoice descriptions, click on the 'print preview' button at the bottom of the screen. You can now see a complete sales invoice.
7. If you want to send a print of this invoice to customer then click on the 'Save and Close' button.
8. In case you want to send the invoice directly to the customer then click on the 'drop-down arrow on 'Save and Close'

button. Then select 'Save and Send'.

9. Compose your email and enter the email address and subject and click 'Send'.

- ## Receive Payments

    1. From the 'customer center' select 'Receive Payments'.
    2. A 'receive payments' window will open.
    3. Now click on the 'received from' drop-down arrow. It will open a customer list.
    4. Select the customer from this list and it will open the list of all outstanding invoices at the bottom of the window.
    5. Enter the payment amount in the Amount box.

6. Enter the date in the date box.
7. Select the payment type from the PMT. Method dropdown.
8. In case of credit card payment enter the card number and the expiration date in the relevant boxes.
9. Select the account in which you want to deposit payment from the 'Deposit To' drop-down arrow.
10. Select the invoice to which you want to apply for the payment. Otherwise, QuickBooks will select the earliest invoice by default.
11. Click on 'Save and Close' now. You have successfully applied

for the payment from customers in QuickBooks.

How To Create and Send Sales Receipts?

1. Click on customer>Sales receipts.
2. A Sales receipt template will open on the screen
3. Enter the customer name, email, billing address, receipt date, reference, and deposit number and select payment type.
4. Enter other details including product/service name, description, quantity, rate and amount.
5. After entering all the descriptions of Sales receipts,

click on the 'print preview' button at the bottom of the screen. You can now see a complete sales receipt.

6. If you want to send a print of this sales receipt to customer then click on the 'Save and Close' button.
7. In case you want to send the sales receipts directly to the customer then click on the 'drop-down arrow on the 'Save and Close' button. Then select 'Save and Send'.
8. Compose your email and enter the email address and subject and click 'Send'.

- ## How To Customize Your Sales Forms

    1. Click on Gear Icon>Account Setting>Sales Tab.
    2. Select 'customize the look and feel'. From here you can custom form styles and add a new one as well.
    3. Now custom style, appearance, header, footer, and the activity table.
    4. After the changes click on 'Print and Preview'.

CHAPTER FIVE - Manage Your Bills and Other Expenses

Set-up Vendor Center

- **How To Create a Bill?**
    1. Navigate to the vendor center from the homepage and click.
    2. Select 'Bill' under the vendor's section.
    3. From the vendor list select the supplier whose bill is this.
    4. In the case of a new supplier, click on +Add new.

5. And click 'Save'.
6. Now enter other details of the bills including the terms, bill date, and due date.
7. From the 'Account' drop-down menu, select the account from which you want to make payment. And add its description.
8. Click 'save and new' in case you want to create another bill.
9. Click 'Save and close' to proceed.

- **Enter Expense Type as per the Transaction**
    1. Navigate back to the Vendor center.
    2. Select 'expense' under the vendor section.
    3. An 'expense' template will open.
    4. Select the payee from the list of the supplier or click on +Add New to enter a new payee/supplier.
    5. Click 'Save' to continue.
    6. Fill in the relevant fields on the expense template the same as you did to create the bill.

7. Now enter the account details. Choose an account type from the Account drop-down menu and description.
8. Enter the payment date.
9. Select the payment type/method.
10. Now choose the 'expense' type from the category of the account.
11. Split the purchase/expense categories in case you have paid for the different items in one single payment.
12. Add the description and amount of the payment.

13. Click 'Save and New' in case you want to enter another expense.
14. Click 'Save and Close' in case you don't want to create another expense transaction.

- How To Pay Multiple Bills?
    1. Navigate back to the vendor center and select the 'pay bills'
    2. Choose the account type from the Account drop-down menu from which you want to make payments.
    3. Enter the payment date.
    4. In case you chose a checking accounting then

enter Starting Check number as well.
5. Now from the list of expenses select all the expenses you want to pay.
6. Then enter the payment amount for the whole transaction.
7. Click 'Save' or 'Save and Print' or Save and Close'.

- How to Create a Check to Pay the Bill?
  1. Click on the create icon and select 'check'.
  2. Select the Payee you from the payee drop-down menu.

3. In the case of the outstanding payee, an 'Add to Check' panel will open.
    a. From this panel select 'Add to pay an open bill' or 'Add all to pay all open bills'.
    b. Then apply for any 'vendor credit'.
4. Select the account from the 'Account' drop-down menu from which you want to pay the bill.
5. Assign a location to the bill from the 'Location' drop-down menu.

6. Now enter the payment amount of the Check.
7. In case of multiple bills check, select all the bills you want to pay with this check under the outstanding transaction section.
   a. Enter the overall transaction amount.
   b. Split the total check amount by bills.
8. Select a Print check.
9. Select Save and close. Or select Save and new to create a new check for another bill.

- **How To Print Check Bills in Batch?**
  1. Click on banking>Write check.
  2. Select the 'print later' checkbox, right next to the print icon.
  3. Close the 'write check' window.
  4. Click on 'file' from the menu bar.
  5. Then select 'print forms'.
  6. Select 'paychecks' or checks.
  7. Choose your bank account.
  8. Check all the checks you want to print in a batch.

9. Enter the first check number.
10. Click 'Ok'.
11. Choose the check style such as Voucher, standard or wallet.
12. Then 'click' print icon.

13.

CHAPTER SIX - Financial Reporting

- Prepare Profit and Loss / Balance Sheet

- Profit and Loss Statement

You have to **create a list of classes** including income, expenses, cost of goods sold etc in order to generate a p&l.

1. Open QuickBooks.
2. Click on the 'Edit' tab from the QuickBooks menu.
3. Now click on the preference>Accounting>

Company Preferences box.
4. Now check in the 'use class tracking'>prompt to assign classes' boxes.
5. Click 'Ok'.
6. From the toolbar click on list>class list from the list drop-down menu.
7. You will see a 'Class' button at the bottom of the page.
8. Click 'class' and then 'new' to generate a new class.
9. Name the class and then click 'Ok.'
10. You can also make subclasses of the class by

checking the 'sub-class' box and selecting a 'primary class' in the text field.

For example, if you have created a class for expenses, you can also create sub-classes (secondary) classes for it such as rent, admin expenses, selling and distribution expenses, etc.

11. Now allocate an expense (bill) or income (invoice) to each class.
12. Click the 'class' drop-down arrow and select the class you want to assign a specific invoice or expense bill.

Once you are done with class creation, the next step is:

13. Click on the 'File' tab from the QuickBooks menu.
14. Now click on the 'Account' drop-down menu and select the account from which you want to create the p&l statement.
15. Click 'reports' and then chose 'Company and Financial'.
16. Now select the 'profit and loss by the class' from the drop-down

menu. You can also type 'profit and loss by class' phrase into a QuickBooks search bar to do this.

17. Click 'Ok' and your report will be generated.

In case you forgot to assign a class to a specific expense or income, QuickBooks will remind you before generating the report. It will mark all the non-allocated items as 'unclassified' class. You can assign the class to unclassified p&l items using 16 and 17 respectively.

QuickBooks

- <u>Balance Sheet</u>

    1. Open the QuickBooks software.
    2. Click on the 'File' tab from the menu.
    3. Click on 'Accounts' drop-down arrow and select the account for whom you want to pull out the balance sheet.
    4. Now click on 'reports' drop-down menu and then select 'Company and Financial'.
    5. A list of various types of balance sheets will open. You can also type the 'balance sheet' phrase

into QuickBooks search bar to do this.
6. Select the type of balance sheet that you want to prepare for the current period.
7. Click 'Ok' and it will create the balance sheet report for you.

- Manage Accounts Receivable

- **Summary of Sales by Customers**
   1. Click on the 'reports' tab on the left of the Navigation bar.
   2. Click on All Reports> Sales Review option.

3. Now select the 'Sales by Customer Summary' within the 'Sales review' section.
4. A report will pop up now.
5. Change the 'This-month-to-date' to 'this-quarter-to-date' or 'this-year-to-date' according to your needs.
6. Click 'Run Report'.
7. It will create a summary report of the sales by customer.

- [Details of Sales by Customers]()
    1. Click on the 'reports' tab on the left of the Navigation bar.
    2. Click on All Reports> Sales Review option.
    3. Now select the 'Sales by Customer Details' within the 'Sales review' section.
    4. A report will pop up now.
    5. Change the 'This-month-to-date' to 'this-quarter-to-date' or 'this-year-to-date' according to your needs.

6. Now click the 'customize' button on the left corner.
7. Chose the relevant rows and columns by 'month'.
8. Click 'run report' at the bottom right corner of the report window.
9. Now analyze your sales by customer report.

- <u>Details on Unbilled Charges:</u>

1. Click on the 'reports' tab on the left of the Navigation bar.
2. Click on All Reports> Sales Review option.

3. Type 'Unbilled Charges' in the report window search box.
   4. Select 'billable expense charge' and then click 'Bill' reference on the top of the 'Date' tab.

- ## Manage Accounts Payables

  - ### Summary of Accounts Payables:

    1. Click on the 'reports' tab on the left of the Navigation bar.
    2. Click on All Reports> Vendors and Payables option.

3. Now select the 'Vendor Balance Summary' within the 'Vendors and Payables' section.
4. Click 'run report'.

- Review Purchases and Other Expenses:

  1. Click on the 'reports' tab on the left of the Navigation bar.
  2. Click on All Reports> Review Expenses & Purchases option.
  3. Now select 'Expenses by Vendor Summary'.
  4. Click the 'customize' button at the top left of the screen.

5. Click 'Sort by' drop-down menu and select sort by 'total' in descending order.
6. Now click 'run report'.

- <u>Transaction List by Vendor:</u>

  1. From QuickBooks homepage click on expenses>vendors.
  2. Click on the 'transaction list' tab.
  3. From here you can do the following:
     - Edit the vendor's profile via the 'Edit' option.
     - Create new bills, expenses, purchase

orders, checks or vendor credit via 'create new'.
- Hide the irrelevant transaction via filters.
- Take batch actions for a specific transaction using the batch action drop-down menu.

Manage Payrolls:

1. Go to the 'Employee' center from the QuickBooks navigation menu.
2. Click the 'Add payroll' or 'get set up' button.

3. Answer and respond to the questions regarding the previous payrolls.
4. A window 'tell us about your employee' will open.
5. Click on 'Add employee' at the bottom left corner.
6. Enter and complete the information of the employee in relevant fields.
7. Now go back to the 'employee' center.
8. Click 'Run payroll" located in the upper right corner.
9. Add the hours worked by the employee and other relevant information.
10. Review the report and then click 'run report'.

- ## Manage Sales tax:

    1. Click on the 'reports' tab on the left of the Navigation bar.
    2. Click on All Reports> Vendors and Payables option.
    3. Now select the 'sales tax liability' or 'sales tax revenue summary within the 'Vendors and Payables' section.
    4. Click 'run report'.

- ## Inventory and Finished Goods Management

    1. Go to reports>inventory>inventory valuation summary.

- Statement of Cash Flows:

- ☐ Cash Flow Forcast Report:
    1. Open the QuickBooks software.
    2. Click on the 'File' tab from the menu.
    3. Now click on 'reports' drop-down menu and then select 'Company and Financial'.
    4. Select 'Cash flow forecast.
    5. You can customize the specifications of the reports. Once you are done you compare your projections with previous cash flows.

- Cash Flow Statement For Current Period:
    1. Click on the 'File' tab from the menu.
    2. Now click on the 'reports' drop-down menu and then select 'All reports'.
    3. Click 'business overview > statement of cashflows.
- Aging Analysis of Accounts Receivables and Payables
    - Aging Analysis of Accounts Receiveable:
        1. Click on the 'reports' tab on the left of the Navigation bar.

2. Click on All Reports> Sales Review option.
3. Now select the 'Sales by Customer Details' within the 'Sales review' section.
4. A report window will pop up now.
5. Now type 'Aging' in the report window search box.
6. Choose 'A/R Aging Summary' from the drop-down menu.

7. It will categorize the invoices into four columns:
    - ❖ Column 1-30 for 'current' invoices.
    - ❖ Column 31-60 for 'late' invoice.
    - ❖ Column 61-90 for 'extremely late' invoices.
    - ❖ Column 91 and Over for 'delinquent' invoices.

- [Aging Analysis of Accounts Payables:](#)
    1. Click on the 'reports' tab on the left of the Navigation bar.
    2. Click on All Reports> Vendors and Payables option.
    3. Now select the 'A/P Aging Summary' within the 'Vendors and Payables' section.
    4. Now click on 'customize repost' and apply 'Filters'.

5. Click 'job type' under the filter section.
6. From the 'job type,' drop-down menu select as 'multiple job types' and then select as many job types for which you want a summary report.
7. Click 'Ok'.

CHAPTER SEVEN - Different Versions of QuickBooks

- ## QuickBooks Self-employed

    1. This is the newest version of the QuickBooks family.
    2. QuickBooks has mainly introduced this version for Freelancers.
    3. QuickBooks Self-employed comes with strong tax support.
    4. Its features include quarterly tax calculator feature, expense tracking, deductions, invoicing, a few reports, and distinguish

between personal expenses and business expenses.
5. This is not an accounting software but this version calculates the tax using 'cash basis accounting'.
6. It also has a Turbotax integration and a great UI.
7. There are precisely two packages including $10/month and $17/month.
8. It is a cloud-based application so hence you don't need to install it.
9. This version of QuickBooks is compatible with all computer devices, mobile phone devices, and tablets.

10. It is ideal for independent contractors, e-commerce site owners, freelancers, and self-employed persons.
11. It allows access to a single user only.

- **QuickBooks Online:**
  - **Features Of QuickBooks Online:**

Just like any other accounting software or tool, QuickBooks Online also offers some basic accounting tools. But in addition to these basic tools, QuickBooks also has some advanced features.

QuickBooks

- <u>Basic Features:</u>
  - **<u>Cloud Accounting:</u>**
    QuickBooks has made it possible to access your account 24/7, and from any place. Cloud accounting feature not only enables the users to access their accounts anytime, anywhere but they can also manage and organize their accounts through computers, tablets, and mobile phones.
  - **<u>Expense Tracking:</u>**
    With QuickBooks, you can easily track and record your expenses. It

makes your tax return filling a lot easier. But what's new about this feature is that you can screenshot as well as save your receipts with QuickBooks Online mobile app.

- **Invoicing:**

What use of accounting software without invoicing feature? Well, QuickBooks understand the importance of invoices and hence allows you to create and custom not only professional invoices and receipts but enables you to send these and estimates with-in minutes.

- **Accounting Reports:** This feature is one of the critical features. It helps you to overlook the overall performance of your business, plus you can create and compare your current financial reports with previous ones. And due to this feature, you can also keep track of your overdue and delayed invoices.

- **CashFlow Management:**
 You can manage your cash inflows and outflows much better with QuickBooks. It has a feature that allows you to enter all your vendor bills and schedule your periodic payments.
- **Account Access:**
 Be it you or your accountant, with QuickBooks your accounts and records are accessible from remote. And hence this feature helps you and your team, work together.

- **Data Security:**

  You can enter your bank details and financial information without worrying about data theft. QuickBooks uses bank-level security that is 128-bit SSL encryption to ensure the safety of your data.

- **Data Backup:**

  Automatic and daily data back-up is another fine feature of QuickBooks. Your data is always up-to-date without any hassle or effort.

- **Free and Unlimited Support:**

Unlike the other accounting software, QuickBooks offers the best support services so far. If you are stuck or confused about something you can ask for help from QuickBooks support. In my experience, I have found their support, very cooperative and understanding. They promptly respond to your queries if you contact then from Monday to

Friday between 7:00 am and 12:00 am (GMT+8).

- **Additional Features:**

If you are thinking that QuickBooks is just about those basic features, then let me assure you that this accounting software is far more than these features. Here is a list of all the other features which are offered by QuickBooks.

1. QuickBooks allows you to import and export data from Excel Spreadsheets.
2. It also helps you with the local tax rates configuration.
3. Not only you can manage your bills but also pay them withQuickBooks.

4. You have full control over who and what he can access.
5. You can handle multiple currencies all at once.
6. QuickBooks also differentiate the supplier bills and payments from other payments, making it easier for you to manage.
7. You can track your inventory/stocks.
8. It offers tools to create a budget so that you can forecast your inflows (income) and outflows (expenses).
9. It enables you to track all your income and expenses as per the job or project (individual type).
10. You can track your sales and overall profitability separately

for all your locations/places of operation.

What features you are going to get depends on what package you select. You can get a free thirty days trial on all three packages. Plus QuickBooks also offers a 50% discount for the first six months on all packages. Amazing! QuickBooks, offers three different packages, including

- **<u>SimpleStart:</u>**
  It is the most basic package. This package offers all the basic features plus two additional features including the data import and export from

excel sheets and local tax rates configuration.

Under this package, only a single user can use the Online QuickBooks simultaneously at a time. Further, you can have up to 14 built-in business reports in SimpleStart basic package.

This package is the most economical package of QuickBooks that costs $15.00/moUSD. This package is good for beginners, small scale freelancers, and self-employed persons.

- **Essentials:**

The second package comes with essential accounting features that include all the basic features and six additional features. The additional features which you could enjoy in this package includes local tax rate configuration, data import, and export from excel, separate management, and payment of supplier bills and other bills, multiple currencies option, and control over the access.

Unlike the simplest package, 3 users can simultaneously use QuickBooks Online under the

Essentials Package. Plus, this package offers more than 40 built-in Business reports for its users. The whole package costs around $23/mo USD. This is quite a good package for small businesses, entrepreneurs or even a Single Member Company.

I personally chose the essential package and for someone like me, this package is perfect. It has enough features to help you manage my cash flows. I can track my expenses, income quite easily. But if you are thinking that I started with this package then you are wrong.

So here comes another tip from my experience, if you have a small business and you want to manage your accounts on your own, but have no idea how to use it; then first take the thirty days Trial SimpleStart. Trust me, it will help you learn a lot about QuickBooks and how to use its tools to manage your accounts.

- **<u>Plus:</u>**

The third and the last package offered by QuickBooks is the 'Plus'. You get all the features and tools as offered in the other two packages. But what makes this package special is that it has even the large scale business and companies can use this to keep track of their transactions and other financial information.

It is because, in this package, QuickBooks provides tools to track inventory/Stocks and allows you to create budgeted financial statements. Moreover, the reason why I am saying that this package is helpful even for large scale businesses is that QuickBooks has all the features as per the needs and requirements of such businesses.

Obviously there are multiple projects and jobs when we move up to large scale businesses. Which is why QuickBooks has introduced features that helps to track your business income, expenses, sales, and overall business profitability according to individual jobs, projects and business locations.

The cost of this package is just $31.00/mo USD. in addition to all the features, Plus packages provide simultaneous access to QuickBooks online up to 25 persons and come with 65+

built-in business reports. Which is why this package is absolutely perfect for large scale businesses as well.

- ## QuickBooks for Desktop/Mac:

QuickBooks offers four different products for Desktop and Mac computers. Each Desktop/mac product is designed for different companies and enterprises. QuickBooks Desktop/mac is the actual accounting software that offers all the features. This version is ideal for small to medium-size businesses and companies. To enjoy the features of Quickbook desktop/mac you have to purchase it first. After which you can download and install it.

QuickBooks

- **QuickBooks Pro:**

1. QuickBooks Pro is ideal for businesses and companies having annual revenue of up to $1million.
2. It costs $2999.5 USD.
3. QuickBooks pro is accessible to 3 persons/users at a time.
4. It helps to track and manage inventory, sales tax, and multiple currencies.
5. You can get 100+ templates of detailed business reports.

- **QuickBooks Premier:**

1. The target users of this version are the non-profit organizations, wholesalers, professional service providers, manufacturers, and retail businesses.
2. This costs you $499.95 USD.
3. It allows access to 5 users at a time.

4. It offers features to track and manage inventory, sales tax, multiple currencies, create sales order and bill of materials.
5. In addition to these features, QuickBooks premier also offers Industry-specific versions as well.
6. It contains 150+ detailed business report templates.

- QuickBooks Enterprise:

1. Any company or business that has an annual revenue of more than $1million must use this version of QuickBooks.
2. The purchase price for this version is $1155/year USD.
3. Up to 30 users can use QuickBooks Enterprise simultaneously.

4. It has all the features of the first two versions. But in addition to those features, you can also have an Accountant toolbox as well as manage fixed assets.
5. It provides more than 150 detailed business reports.

QuickBooks Accountant:

1. As the name indicates, this QuickBooks Desktop product is ideal for Bookkeepers and Accountants.
2. It costs $349/year USD.
3. It has all the features of QuickBooks Enterprise.
4. With this version of QuickBooks, you can toggle to other editions.
5. Plus it has a batch void/delete transaction feature as well.

6. It offers more than 150 business reports.

CHAPTER EIGHT - Key Shortcuts For Using QuickBooks

- ## QuickBooks Desktop (Pro, Premier, Enterprise)
  - ### Open, set up, and close QuickBooks

Action	Keyboard shortcut
To Direct Open your Company File	Hold Alt after you open your company file on the Open Company window

Close QuickBooks Program	Alt + F4
Open QuickBooks Payroll Service Keys	Ctrl + K
Format Year-to-Date Payroll Amounts	Select the Help menu and then About QuickBooks. When the product screen appears, Ctrl + Alt + Y.

QuickBooks

- Navigate around QuickBooks

Activity	Keyboard shortcut
Direct Open the Help window	F1
Close current window	Esc
Direct Open the Product Information window	F2 or Ctrl+1
Navigate the Find Transaction window	Ctrl+F
Navigate the Search window	F3 or Ctrl+2
Navigate Tech	F2, for the

Info/Tech Help window	Product Info window Then F3

- <u>Start a new task anywhere in QuickBooks</u>

Activity	Keyboard shortcut
Generate a new invoice	Ctrl + I
Generate a new check	Ctrl + W

Go to Customer Center	Ctrl + J
Go the Chart of Accounts	Ctrl + A
Open an Account Register	Ctrl + R, then select an account. If you are in an account register, select a transaction and press Ctrl+G. This

	opens the register for the associated "transfer" account.

- <u>Data fields on forms</u>

Activity	**Keyboard shortcut**
Raise or Reduce the amount	+ or -
Jump to the next data field	Tab

Jump to the previous data field	Shift + Tab
Copy, paste, undo, cut	Ctrl + C, Ctrl + V, Ctrl + Z, Ctrl + X

- <u>Date fields on forms</u>

Activity	**Keyboard shortcut**
Open calendar	Alt + ↓
Move Advance a	+

day	
Move Back a day	-
Move to today	T
Move to the first day of the week	W
Move to the last day of the week	K

Move to the same day next week	]
Move to the same day last week	[
Move to the first day of the month	M
Move to the last day of the month	H

Move to the same day of the month next month	;
Move to the same day of the month last month	' (apostrophe)
Move to the first day of the year (Jan 1)	Y

QuickBooks

- <u>Forms and transactions (invoices, expenses, etc)</u>

Activity	Keyboard shortcut
Record or save a transaction	Enter
Add a new transaction line	Ctrl + Ins
Remove selected transaction line	Ctrl + Del

Copy a transaction line	Highlight a transaction line, then press Ctrl + Alt + Y. *Only available in QuickBooks 2018 and later.
Paste a transaction line	Highlight a blank transaction line, then press Ctrl + Alt + V. *Only

	available in QuickBooks 2018 and later.
Move to the next or previous transaction line	↑ or ↓
Unfold the full list for the selected drop-down menu.	Highlight the drop-down menu, then press Ctrl + L. Press Ctrl + U to add a

	selected item from the list to your open form.
Move between pages on forms and reports	Page Up or Page Down
Save and close the current form	Alt + S
Navigate to	Alt + P

QuickBooks

your last open form of the same type	
Save and go to the next form of the same type	Alt + N
Print form (or list)	CTRL + P
Memorize current form and its transactions	Ctrl + M

Open Memorized Transaction List	Ctrl + T
Open current form's transaction history	Ctrl + H
Open current form's transaction journal	Ctrl + Y

QuickBooks

- Lists (Customer Center, Account Register, Item List, etc)

Activity	Keyboard shortcut
Move to the register or list's first or last item	Ctrl + Page Up or Ctrl + Page Down
Generate a new item on a list	Ctrl + N
Edit an item on a new or	Ctrl + E

old list	
Delete an item on a new or old list	Ctrl + D
Test Run a Quick Report for an item on a list	Ctrl + F6
Refresh list	F5

QuickBooks Desktop for Mac

- Open, set up, and close QuickBooks

Activity	Keyboard shortcut
Make a new company file	Option + Command + N
Navigate to a company file	Command + O
Close a company file	Option + Command + W
Shut QuickBooks	Command + W

- **Navigate around QuickBooks**

Action	Keyboard shortcut
Open the Help window	Command + ?
Minimize current window	Command + M
Shut current window	ESC

Shut all windows	Shift + select window
Open Preferences	Command + , (comma)
Open Contextual menu	Hold Control, then select the object
Open the Product Information window	Command + 1

Open the Find Transaction window	Command + F
Hide QuickBooks	Command + H

- <u>Data fields on forms</u>

Activity	Keyboard shortcut
Move to the next data field	Tab

Move to the previous data field	Shift + Tab
Copy, paste, undo, cut	Command + C, Command + V, Command + Z, Command + X

- Date fields on forms

Action	Keyboard shortcut

Move Advance a day	+
Move a day Back	-
Move to today	T
Move to the first day of the week	W
Move to the last day of the week	K

Move to the first day of the month	M
Move to the last day of the month	H
Move to the first day of the year (Jan 1)	Y
Move to the last day of the year (Dec 31)	R

- <u>Forms and transactions (invoices, expenses, etc)</u>

Activity	Keyboard shortcut
Add a new transaction line	Command + Y
Remove selected transaction line	Command + B
Copy a transaction line	Option + Command + C

Unroll the full list for the selected drop-down menu	Highlight the drop-down menu, then press Command + L
Move between pages on forms and reports	FN + ↑ or ↓
Print form (or list)	Command + P
Memorize current form and its transactions	Command and + (plus)

Open current form's transaction history	Command + U

- [Lists (Customer Center, Account Register, Item List, etc)](#)

Activity	Keyboard shortcut
Move to the register or list's first or last item	Command + PgUporCommand + PgDn
Create a new item on a list	Command + N

Edit an item on a list	Command + E
Delete an item on a list	Command + D
Open an Account Register	Command + R, then select an account

CONCLUSION

In the final, I just want to say that QuickBooks is just another software that has its own manual. If you are thinking that you can't learn QuickBooks or its hard to use this brilliant accounting software, then put that thought aside! Hundreds of thousands of individuals and companies, including me, use this accounting software. And it is definitely not hard to understand and use QuickBooks tools.

With proper guidance and manual, it's a matter of a week to master QuickBooks. But what really matters is how you use this software and its tools to do your regular accounting tasks! After using QuickBooks myself, I can confidently say that you don't need to spend your money on Accountants. I am referring this to the small businesses, entrepreneurs and freelancers.

Trust me, you can save a lot of money by just learning how to use QuickBooks. This accounting software provides all the basic, essential and advanced accounting tools to its customers. So that you can keep track of your business transactions without any stress.

In a nutshell, QuickBooks is an amazing accounting software and its simple practice. And with regular and daily practice you can unlock and reveal new ways of handling your business transactions without any stress!

ABOUT THE AUTHOR

Lucas Calderon is an experienced economist, financial planner, and a real estate investor. His zeal and passion is to educate property investors on the necessary steps that will help them to harness their incomes and economic resources to build a better and an appealing lifestyle devoid of frustrations and suffering after retirement.

As an economist, he is committed to exposing the risks and dangers of having poor or no plans for retirement through his books, journals, seminar, and symposiums.

INDEX

A

access, 2, 26, 88, 89, 96, 99, 103, 105
Accountant toolbox, 107
accounting, 1, ii, iii, 1, 2, 14, 58, 87, 88, 89, 90, 94, 95, 99, 104, 138, 139
accounting tools, iii, 88, 139
Accounts, 1, 5, 6, 13, 14, 15, 16, 17, 36, 37, 38, 39, 44, 69, 70, 74, 81, 84, 113
activity, 53
annual revenue, 105, 106

B

balance sheets, 69
beginner, 13
beginners, iii, 4, 98
business, i, ii, iii, 1, 5, 8, 9, 14, 15, 16, 19, 23, 24, 29, 32, 81, 87, 91, 98, 101, 102, 103, 104, 105, 106, 107, 108, 139

C

cash, i, 15, 19, 80, 87, 92, 100

Cash Flow, 1, 80, 81
cashflows, 81
categories, 41, 57
categorize, 83
cloud, 87
companies, iii, 102, 104, 105, 138
Company, 1, 2, 3, 7, 8, 12, 13, 22, 65, 67, 69, 80, 100, 109
computer, 87
configuration, 95, 98, 99
credit, 16, 17, 19, 37, 38, 44, 45, 46, 50, 60, 77
currencies, 96, 99, 105, 106
customers, 10, 19, 23, 27, 47, 51, 139
customize, 1, 14, 15, 17, 20, 21, 22, 53, 73, 75, 80, 84

D

Data Backup, 93
deductions, 86

E

e-commerce, 88
employee, 10, 78
entrepreneurs, iii, 100, 139
Essentials, 99, 100
expense, 16, 18, 56, 57, 58, 66, 68, 74, 86
expenses, 1, i, ii, 16, 23, 59, 64, 66, 76, 87, 89, 96, 100, 103, 119, 134
Expenses, 1, 54, 75

F

features, iii, 1, 14, 21, 22, 86, 88, 91, 95, 97, 99, 100, 101, 102, 103, 104, 106, 107
filling, 90
financial, i, ii, iii, 15, 23, 29, 91, 93, 102, 140
fixed assets, 15, 107
freelancers, iii, 88, 98, 139

G

guidance, 138
guide, 1, iii

H

homepage, 22, 36, 47, 54, 76

I

industry, 5, 6, 14
inflows, i, 19, 92, 96
information, 1, 4, 5, 8, 9, 10, 12, 13, 27, 33, 34, 78, 93, 102
integration, 87
inventory, 12, 79, 96, 102, 105, 106
invoices, 1, 19, 49, 83, 90, 91, 119, 134
invoicing, 86, 90

J

Job Costing', 29
Job Tracking, 29

L

learning, 139

M

management, 99
manufacturers, 105
menu, 3, 5, 17, 19, 20, 21, 22, 23, 28, 29, 30, 32, 34, 38, 43, 55, 57, 58, 59, 60, 62, 64, 65, 67, 68, 69, 76, 77, 80, 81, 82, 85, 110, 121, 129, 135
money, iii, 139

N

Navigation bar, 70, 72, 73, 74, 75, 79, 81, 84
non-profit, 105

O

organizations, 105

P

Package. Plus, 100
packages, 87, 97, 101, 103
Payables, 1, 74, 75, 79, 81, 84
payrolls, 78
performance, ii, 2, 29, 91
phone devices, 87
practice, iii, 139
Preview, 5, 53
purchase, 1, 57, 76, 104, 106
Purchases, 1, 75

Q

QuickBooks, 1, ii, iii, 1, 2, 3, 4, 6, 7, 8, 13, 14, 17, 18, 19, 20, 21, 22, 23, 24, 26, 29, 31, 35, 36, 37, 38, 39, 45, 47, 50, 51, 64, 67, 68, 69, 70, 76, 77, 80, 86, 87, 88, 89, 90, 92, 93, 94, 95, 96, 97, 98, 99, 101, 102, 103, 104, 105, 106, 107, 109, 110, 111,112, 120, 121, 127, 128, 130, 138, 139

R

receipts, 43, 51, 52, 90
reference, 47, 51, 74
Reports, 1, 21, 70, 72, 73, 74, 75, 79, 82, 84, 91
Run Report', 71

S

Sales review', 71, 72, 82
sales tax, 79, 105, 106

single user, 88, 98
software, ii, iii, 1, 2, 14, 69, 80, 87, 88, 90, 94, 95, 104, 138, 139
success, i
Summary', 71, 75, 82, 84

T

tablets, 87, 89
tax rates, 95, 98
tracking, 23, 65, 86
transaction, 17, 21, 37, 39, 40, 41, 42, 45, 58, 59, 61, 76, 77, 107, 113, 119, 120, 121, 124, 134, 136
transactions, 1, 17, 18, 21, 37, 38, 39, 102, 119, 123, 134, 135, 139
Turbotax, 87

V

vendors, 10, 23, 34, 76

W

wholesalers, 105

Made in the USA
Monee, IL
16 March 2021